I am a Vulture

Heather Kissock

www.av2books.com

AV² provides enriched content that supplements and complements this book. Weigl's AV² books strive to create inspired learning and engage young minds in a total learning experience.

Your AV² Media Enhanced books come alive with...

Go to www.av2books.com, and enter this book's unique code.

BOOK CODE

K 8 3 5 3 7 3

AV² by Weigl brings you media enhanced books that support active learning.

Audio
Listen to sections of the book read aloud.

Video
Watch informative video clips.

Embedded Weblinks
Gain additional information for research.

Try This!
Complete activities and hands-on experiments.

Key Words
Study vocabulary, and complete a matching word activity.

Quizzes
Test your knowledge.

Slide Show
View images and captions, and prepare a presentation.

... and much, much more!

Published by AV² by Weigl
350 5ᵗʰ Avenue, 59ᵗʰ Floor New York, NY 10118
Website: www.av2books.com

Library of Congress Cataloging-in-Publication Data

Names: Kissock, Heather.
Title: Vulture / Heather Kissock.
Description: New York, NY : AV2 by Weigl, 2017. l Series: I am l Includes
  bibliographical references and index.
Identifiers: LCCN 2015037943l ISBN 9781489641250 (hard cover : alk. paper) l
  ISBN 9781489641267 (soft cover : alk. paper) l ISBN 9781489641274
  (single-user ebook) l ISBN 9781489641281 (multi-user ebook)
Subjects: LCSH: Vultures--Juvenile literature.
Classification: LCC QL696.F32 K57 2015 l DDC 598.9/2--dc23
LC record available at http://lccn.loc.gov/2015037943

Printed in the United States of America in Brainerd, Minnesota
1 2 3 4 5 6 7 8 9 0 19 18 17 16 15

102015
151015

Editor: Heather Kissock   Art Director: Terry Paulhus

The publisher acknowledges Corbis, Minden Pictures, and Alamy as the primary image suppliers for this title.

I am a Vulture

In this book, I will teach you about

- myself

- my food

- my home

- my family

and much more!

I am a vulture.

5

I like
to eat leftovers.

6

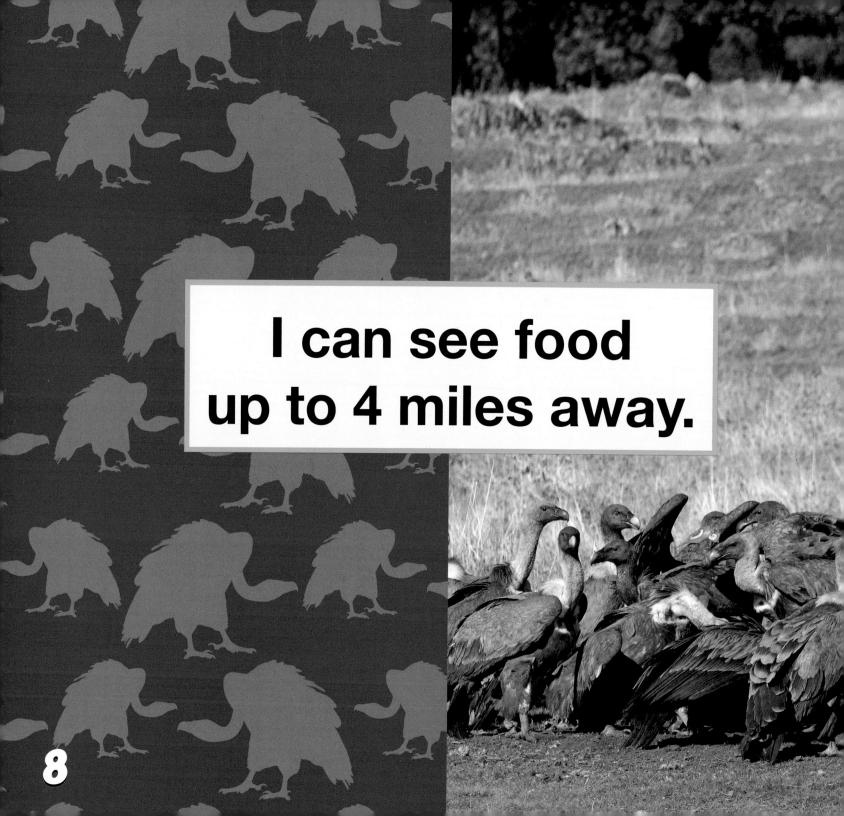

I can see food
up to 4 miles away.

8

I can fly
without flapping
my wings.

10

I use my curved beak to rip my food apart.

12

13

I share my food
with others.

I store extra food
in my throat.

I am almost always the only chick in my nest.

18

I help to stop disease from spreading.

I am a vulture.

VULTURE FACTS

These pages provide detailed information that expands on the interesting facts found in the book. They are intended to be used by adults as a learning support to help young readers round out their knowledge of each amazing animal featured in the *I Am* series.

Pages 4–5

I am a vulture. Vultures are birds of prey. There are 23 species of vulture. They are divided into two groups. Old World vultures are found in Asia, Europe, and Africa. New World vultures live in the Americas. Antarctica and Australia are the only continents where vultures do not live.

Pages 6–7

I like to eat leftovers. Vultures are scavengers. They prefer to feed on carrion, or the flesh of dead animals. Vultures are able to overcome the toxic nature of their food due to their highly acidic gastric juices. These juices kill the poisonous bacteria in the carrion. A vulture can eat up to 20 percent of its body weight in one sitting.

Pages 8–9

I can see food up to 4 miles (6.4 kilometers) away. Vultures have excellent eyesight and are able to see food from a great distance. They have large territories as a result and spend much of their time in the air searching for food. A strong sense of smell allows some vultures to detect decaying meat from more than 1 mile (1.6 km) away.

Pages 10–11

I can fly without flapping my wings. Vultures spend much of their flying time riding on thermal currents, which allow them to soar for hours on end without flapping their wings. With a wingspan up to 8.5 feet (2.5 meters), the Ruppell's griffon vulture is one of the highest-flying animals on Earth. It has been seen at elevations higher than Mount Everest.

I use my curved beak to rip my food apart. This beak is also very sharp, which helps the vulture further. A vulture will stick its entire head into its food source to tear meat from within. Its bald neck and head help the bird to keep clean and stay healthy. Vultures can pick a carcass clean in about half an hour. Some vultures will even eat bones.

I share my food with others. While vultures usually search for food independently, they will gather in groups when a food source has been found. Vultures rely on a hierarchy to determine the feeding order. Typically, the larger birds feed first.

I store extra food in my throat. Vultures have a throat pouch for storing food. As vultures do not necessarily feed often, this food can be kept for a later meal. It can also be taken back to the nest and regurgitated to feed the vulture's young.

I am almost always the only chick in my nest. Most vultures will lay only one egg in a year, although some species are known to lay two eggs. Most eggs take about 2 months to hatch. The mother and father work together to raise the chick. They nest in a variety of locations, ranging from trees to cliffs.

I help to stop disease from spreading. By eating rotting animals, vultures help keep the spread of disease under control. Still, vultures are often poisoned by the pesticides and other human-made contaminants that their prey have encountered. There are currently 14 species of vultures listed as endangered or threatened as a result.

KEY WORDS

Research has shown that as much as 65 percent of all written material published in English is made up of 300 words. These 300 words cannot be taught using pictures or learned by sounding them out. They must be recognized by sight. This book contains 25 common sight words to help young readers improve their reading fluency and comprehension. This book also teaches young readers several important content words, such as proper nouns. These words are paired with pictures to aid in learning and improve understanding.

Page	Sight Words First Appearance	Page	Content Words First Appearance
4	a, am, I	4	vulture
6	eat, like, to	6	leftovers
8	away, can, food, miles, see, up	10	wings
10	my, without	12	beak
12	use	16	throat
14	others, with	18	chick, nest
16	in	20	disease
18	almost, always, only, the		
20	from, help, stop